A Joel Schumacher Film

Andrew Lloyd Webber's

The PHANTOM of the OPERA

ISBN 0-634-09909-4

HAL•LEONARD® CORPORATION

7777 W. BLUEMOUND RD. P.O. BOX 13819 MILWAUKEE, WI 53213

Visit Hal Leonard Online at
www.halleonard.com

Andrew Lloyd Webber
앤드류 로이드 웨버
Composer, Book & Orchestrations

앤드류 로이드 웨버는 「Joseph and the Amazing Technicolor Dreamcoat」, 「Jesus Christ Superstar」, 「By Jeeves」, 「Evita」, 「Tell Me on a Sunday」, 「Song & Dance」, 「Cats」, 「Starlight Express」, 「The Phantom of the Opera」, 「Aspects of Love」, 「Sunset Boulevard」, 「Whistle Down the Wind」, 「The Beautiful Game」, 「The Woman in White」의 작곡가이며, 영화 「Gumshoe」, 「The Odessa File」의 사운드트랙을 작곡했다. 또한 「Requiem」으로 그래미상 최우수 컨템퍼러리 부분을 수상하였다.

최근에는 웨스트엔드와 브로드웨이의 프로듀스를 하게 되어, 올리비에 상에 빛나는 「La Bt e」, 「Daisy Pulls It Off」, 2002년 여름에 런던에서 크게 성공한 「Bombay Dreams」도 그가 제작한 작품이다.

토니 상 7회, 그래미 상 3회, 올리비에 상 6회, 골든 그로브 상, 아카데미 상, 인터내셔널 에미 상, 프리미엄 임페리얼 상, 리차드 드쟈스상 뮤지컬 부문을 수상했다.

1992년에는 나이트 작위를 받았으며, 1997년에 1대 귀족의 작위를 수여받았다.

Charles Hart
찰스 하트
Lyrics

런던에서 출생, 메이든헤드와 캠브리지에 다녔다. 뮤지컬 「The Phantom of the Opera」, 「Aspects of Love」, 오페라 「The Vampyr」, 「BBC 2」의 작사를 담당했으며, 텔레비전 「Watching and Split Ends」, 「Granada TV」, 라디오 「Love Songs」, 「BBC Radio 2」 등에서 여러 스타일의 곡의 작사 작곡을 담당했다. 라디오의 코멘테이터, 보컬 트레이닝, 반주, 뮤지컬 연출, 뮤지컬 편곡과 번안의 일인다역을 하고 있으며, 1990년부터 1993년까지는 영국 작사 작곡 아카데미의 평의원으로 임명받았다.

아이버 노벨로 상을 2회 수상했으며, 토니 상에 2회 노미네이트되었다.

Richard Stilgoe
리차드 스틸고
Additional Lyrics & Book

리차드 스틸고는 작년(역주:2004년) 샐리주(州)의 고등사법관을 지냈으며, 전통 있는 집무실에서는 검은 벨벳과 레이스가 있는 집무복을 입고, 범죄율의 저하를 위해 노력하였다.

리버풀에서 자랐으며, 토요일에는 캐빈 클럽에서 연주를 하고 일요일에는 성 아그네스 성가대의 일원으로 찬양 노래를 불렀다. 성가대 공연은 그를 캠브리지로 이끌었고, 그때까지의 음악 경험으로 형성된 사고방식은 모두 부정되었다. 1960년대는 팹(pub), 나이트클럽, 라디오 4의 「투데이 프로그램」에서 자신의 곡을 노래하는 것을 익혔다. 1970년대는 전국방송인 「재즈 라이프」와 자신이 호스트를 담당하는 프로그램의 출연에 힘을 쏟았다. 1980년대는 앤드류 로이드 웨버를 위해 「Cats」의 가사를 아주 약간, 「Starlight Express」 가사의 거의 대부분을, 「The Phantom of the Opera」 가사의 1/3을 썼다. 내셔널유스뮤직 시어터를 위해 「Bodywork」, 「Brilliant The Dinosaur」의 작사 작곡을 담당했다.

1982년에는 피터 스켈런과 함께 로열 버라이어티 퍼포먼스에 출연하였으며, 이런 경험들은 보다 젊은 사람들을 위한 음악을 만들 환경을 제공해야겠다는 결의를 하게 만들었다. 결과적으로는 오르페스 기금을 만들어서 장애자를 위한 음악을 만들 기회를 제공하였고, 올해에는 이 작업을 계속 이어가기 위한 오르페스 센터를 열었다. 정부의 음악기금의 일원으로 11년 동안, 학교의 댄스파티를 로열 알버트 홀에서 주최하고 있다. 올해, 아이들을 위한 「스틸고 토요 콘서트」를 페스티벌홀에서 시작하였으며, 새로운 뮤지컬 「The Day the Earth Moved」를 초연했다.

몬테카를로 라디오 상을 3회, 프리 이탈리아 상, OBE 상을 수상했다.

그의 취미는 건축, 크리켓, 요트, 그리고 5명의 자녀들, 쌍둥이 손자와 함께 새로운 세기(世紀)를 그들과 함께 보내는 것으로 즐거움을 삼고 있다.

Joel Schumacher
조엘 슈마허
Director

작가 겸 감독인 조엘 슈마허는 현재 미국에서 가장 성공한 필름메이커다. 1995년에는 「Batman Forever」가 연간 최대 관객 동원을 기록하였고, 이 모험 판타지 서사시는 세계에서 3억 3,000만 달러를 넘는 흥행수입을 올렸다. 속편은 「Batman and Robin」,조지 클루니를 배트맨 역할에, 아놀드 슈왈츠제네거를 미스터 프리즈 역에 캐스팅했다.

「Batman Forever」 이전에는 비평가들이 절찬했던 수잔 서랜든과 타미 리 존스가 출연, 존 그리샴의 소설을 영화화한 「의뢰인(The Client)」, 1996년에는 존 그리샴의 또 다른 작품을 영화화하여 매튜 맥커너히, 산드라 블록, 사무엘 L.잭슨, 케빈 스페이시가 출연한 「A Time To Kill」을 히트시켰다. 「St. Elmo's Fire」, 「The Lost Boys」, 「Cousins」, 그리고 줄리아 로버츠를 캐스팅해서 연기 뉘앙스 분위기로 주목을 받아 필름 메이커로서의 다재다능함을 발휘한 「Flatliners」, 마찬가지로 줄리아 로버츠를 캐스팅한 「Dying Young」, 마이클 더글라스를 캐스팅하여 논란을 불러일으켰던 「Falling Down」을 감독했다.

1999년에는 니콜라스 케이지 주연의 스릴러 「8mm」, 로버트 드니로와 필립 시모어 호프만의 「Flawless」, 2000년에는 베트남 전쟁 때의 젊은이들의 훈련을 그린 「Tigerland」, 마찬가지로 콜린 파렐 주연의 「Phone Booth」, 2002년에는 제리 브룩하이머와 디즈니가 제작한 안소니 홉킨스와 크리스 록의 「Bad Company」, 제작진이 같은 「Veronica Guerin」을 감독했다.

뉴욕에서 태어나 자랐고, 패션 디자이너 학원에서 디자인과 디스플레이를 공부하여 TV 광고의 아트 디렉터로 엔터테인먼트 업계에 첫발을 내딛었다. 우디 앨런의 화제작 「Sleeper」와 「Interiors」, 허버트 로스의 「The Last of Sheila」에서는 의상 디자이너를 맡았고, 그 후 히트 코메디 「Car Wash」의 각본을 썼다.

다이안 캐논이 주연을 맡고 하베이 카이텔이 갱으로 출연한 TV 영화 「The Virginia Hill Story」로 감독 데뷔를 했다. 릴리 톰린 주연의 「The Incredible Shrinking Woman」으로 영화감독 데뷔를 했고, 이어서 「D.C. Cab」에서는 대본까지 맡았다. 「St. Elmo's Fire」에서는 칼 클렌더와 함께 각본을 썼다. 1988년에는 시카고에서 데이빗 마멧의 통렬한 할리우드 풍자극 「Speed-the-Plow」를 연출, 무대연출가로서도 큰 성공을 거두었다.

Published by

The Really Useful Group Limited

22 Tower Street, London WC2H 9TW

www.reallyuseful.com

ISBN: 0-634-09909-4

This book Copyright 2005 by The Really Useful Group Limited

This edition is comprised of works written for the original stage production of
THE PHANTOM OF THE OPERA
together with three new works, 'The Fairground', 'Journey To The Cemetery'
and 'Learn To Be Lonely', which were specifically written for the movie.

All music arranged by Roger Day except 'The Fairground', 'Journey To The Cemetery'
and 'Learn To Be Lonely', arranged by David Cullen
Music processed by Paul Ewers Music Design

Photographs by Alex Bailey

Book designs by Dewynters, London

THINK OF ME

Music by ANDREW LLOYD WEBBER
Lyrics by CHARLES HART
Additional lyrics by RICHARD STILGOE

Bm
F#7/B
Bm7
When you find___ that once a - gain you long___ to take your heart back and be
E7
D/A
Bm7
Em F#m G A
free, if you ev - er find a mo - ment, spare a thought for
D
Eb
Bb/Eb
Ab/Eb
me.
Bb7/Eb
Eb
Bb/Eb
Ab

Bb   Cm   G/C
We nev-er said___ our love was ev-er-green___ or as un-
Cm7   F   Eb/Bb   Cm7
mf
-chang-ing as the sea, but if you can still re-mem-ber,
f
Fm Gm Ab Bb   Eb Db/Eb Eb7 Ab   Bb/Ab
stop and think of me. Think of all the things we've
Db/Ab   Eb/Bb   Cm7
shared and seen; don't think a-bout the way things

rall.
a tempo
Fm
Bb7
Eb
Bb/Eb
might have been.
Think of me,
think of me wak - ing
mp
Ab/Eb
Bb7/Eb
Eb
Bb/Eb
si - lent and re - signed.
Im - a-gine me,
try-ing too hard_ to
Ab/Eb
Bb7/Eb
Cm
put you from my mind.
Re - call those days,__ look back on
G7/C
Cm7
F7
Eb/Bb
all those times,__ think of the things we'll nev - er do.
There will nev - er be a

Cm7   Fm   Gm   Ab   Bb7   Eb
day   when   I   won't   think   of   you.
Bb/Eb   Ab/Eb   Bb/Eb   Eb
RAOUL
Can it be,
f
mf
Bb/Eb   Ab   Bb7   Cm
can it be Christ - ine
Long a - go___ it seems so
f
mf
G7/C   Cm7   F   Eb/Bb
long a - go,___ how young and in - no - cent we were.   She may not re-mem - ber
f

Cm7   Fm   Gm   Ab   Bb   Cm
CHRISTINE
Flow-ers fade,____ the fruits of
me but I re - mem - ber her.
G7/C   Cm7   F7
sum - mer fade,____ they have their sea - sons, so do we but please
Eb/Bb   Cm7   Fm   Gm   Ab
Cadenza senza mesura
pro-mise me that some - times you will think (ah)____
N.C.   Bb7   Eb
of me.
f   fp   ff

ANGEL OF MUSIC

Music by ANDREW LLOYD WEBBER
Lyrics by CHARLES HART
Additional lyrics by RICHARD STILGOE

CHRISTINE
Gm   E♭   Cm   D⁷/C
Fa - ther once spoke of an an - gel,____ I used to dream he'd ap - pear.
Gm   E♭   Cm⁷   A♭(♭5)   F
Now as I sing I can sense him____ and I know he's here.
B♭   F/B♭   E♭/B♭   F/B♭   B♭   F/B♭   B♭   B♭sus⁴
Here in this room he calls me soft - ly, some-where in - side hid - ing.____
mf
B♭   F/B♭   E♭/B♭   F/B♭   B♭   F/B♭   B♭
Some - how I know he's al - ways with me; he, the un - seen gen - ius.____

Gm
Eb
Cm
D7/C
MEG
Christ-ine, you must have been dream-ing,___ stor-ies like this can't come true.
Gm
Eb
Cm7
Ab(b5)
F
rit.
Christ-ine, you're talk-ing in rid-dles,___ and it's not like you.
a tempo
Db
Ab/Db
Gb/Db
Ab/Db
Db
Ab/Db
Db
Gb/Db
CHRISTINE
CHRISTINE
An-gel of mu - sic, guide and guar-dian, grant to me your glo-ry!___
MEG Who is this an-gel, this
f
poco più mosso
Db
Ab7/Db
Gb/Db
Ab/Db
Db
Ab/Db
Db
CHRISTINE
an-gel of mu - sic, hide no long-er, se-cret and strange an-gel.___ He's

CHRISTINE
rit.
with me ev-en now, all a-round me, it fright-ens me.
MEG
Your hands are cold; your face, Christ-ine, it's white; don't be fright-ened.
pp
a tempo
bass/B♭
PHANTOM
In - so-lent boy, this slave of fash-ion, bask-ing in your glo - ry.
f
B♭ F/B♭ E♭/B♭ F/B♭ B♭ F/B♭ B♭
Ig - nor-ant fool, this brave young suit - or, shar-ing in my tri - umph.
B F♯/B E/B F♯/B B F♯/B B Bsus⁴
CHRISTINE
An - gel, I hear you! Speak, I lis - ten. Stay by my side guide me!
mf

B   F#/B   E/B   F#/B   B   F#/B   B
An - gel, my soul was weak; for-give me! En - ter at last, mas- ter!____

G#m   Emaj7   C#m7   D#/C#
PHANTOM
Flat - ter - ing child, you shall know me,____ see why in sha - dow I hide.

G#m   Emaj7   C#m7   A(b5)   F#
rit.
Look at your face in the mir - ror!____ I am there in - side.

a tempo
D   A/D   G/D   A/D   D   A/D   D   Dsus4
CHRISTINE
An - gel of mu - sic, guide and guar - dian, grant to me your glo - ry!____
f

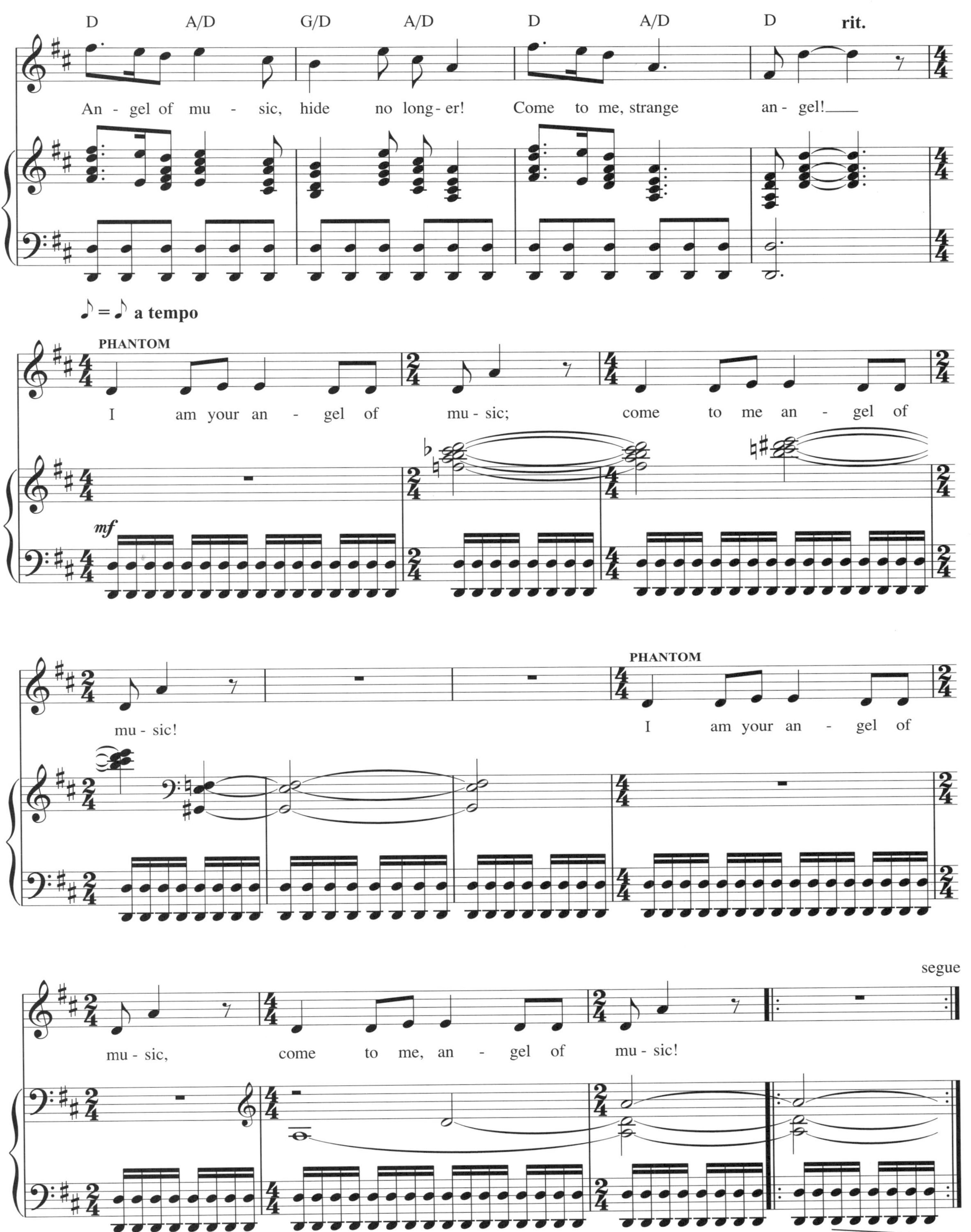

D   A/D   G/D   A/D   D   A/D   D   rit.
An - gel of mu - sic, hide no long - er! Come to me, strange an - gel!
♪ = ♪ a tempo
PHANTOM
I am your an - gel of mu - sic; come to me an - gel of
mf
mu - sic! I am your an - gel of
PHANTOM
mu - sic, come to me, an - gel of mu - sic!
segue

THE PHANTOM OF THE OPERA

Music by ANDREW LLOYD WEBBER
Lyrics by CHARLES HART
Additional lyrics by RICHARD STILGOE & MIKE BATT

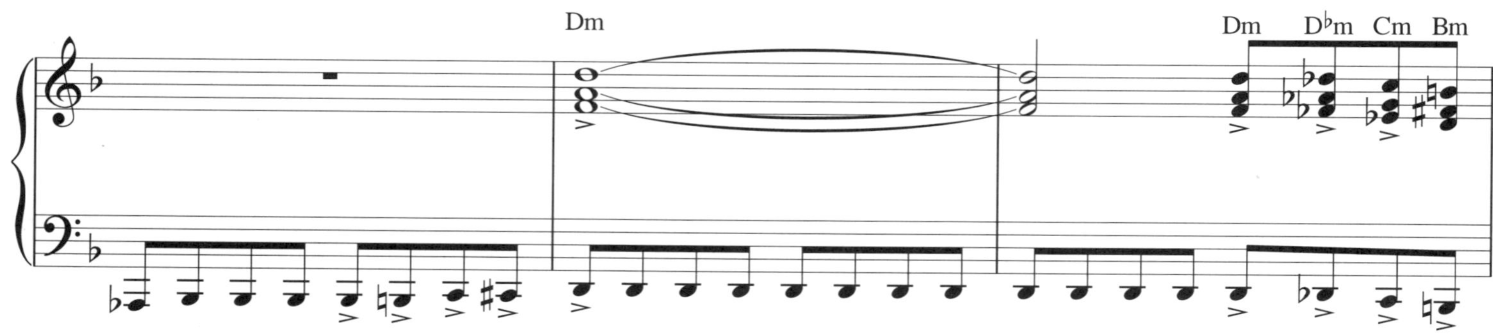

Gsus4   Gm   C   Dm
sang to me,____ in dreams he came, that voice which

Gsus4   Gm   C   Dm
calls to me____ and speaks my name. And do I

B♭maj7   Gm/B♭   C   Dm
dream a - gain?____ for now I find____ the

Dm   B♭○
phan - - tom of the op - er - a is there____ in - side my

Dm
Dm D♭m Cm Bm B♭
mind.
f
A♭ B♭ D♭o Gm
PHANTOM
Sing once a -
mf
Csus⁴ Cm F Gm
gain with me our strange du - et; my pow - er
Csus⁴ Cm F Gm
(8va basso)
ov - er you grows strong - er yet. And though you
26

E♭maj7   Cm/E♭   Gm
turn   from me________   to   glance   be - hind,________________   the

Gm   C°   F♯°
phan - - tom of the op-er-a is   there________________   in - side   your

Gm   (loco) Gm F♯m Fm Em   E♭
mind.________________

D   D7   Em   Asus4   Am
CHRISTINE
Those   who have   seen   your face________

f
mp
27

D/F#   Em   Asus4   Am
draw back in fear. I am the mask you wear,

D/F#   Em/B   Cmaj7   Am/C
PHANTOM
It's me they hear.
PHANTOM & CHRISTINE
Your spi - rit and my voice
My spi - rit and your voice

D   Em   Em
in one com - bined; the phan -
in one com - bined; the phan -

C°   Em
VOICES
- tom of the op-er-a is there inside my mind.
- tom of the op-er-a is there inside your mind.
He's there, the

C
Em
phan - tom of the op - era. Be - ware the
C
phan - tom of the op - era.
Fm
E♭ Fm
PHANTOM
D♭
E♭
In all your fan - ta - sies, you al - ways
Fm
D♭
E♭
CHRISTINE
Fm
knew that man and mys - ter - y were both in you.

PHANTOM & CHRISTINE
D♭maj7
B♭m/D♭
E♭
And in this la - by - rinth where night is
And in this la - by - rinth where night is
mf
Fm
Fm
blind, the phan - - -
blind, the phan - - -
D♭o
- tom of the op - er - a is here in - side my
- tom of the op - er - a is there in - side your
Fm
mind.
mind.
PHANTOM
D♭
(Spoken) Sing, my angel of music!
f

Fm
CHRISTINE
He's there the phan - tom of the
Db
op - era.
Fm
Ah!
Db
PHANTOM
Sing, my angel, sing!
Gm
CHRISTINE
Ah!
Eb
PHANTOM
(1°) Sing for me!

31

1.
2.
CHRISTINE
Am
Ah!
3
F
PHANTOM
Sing, my angel of music!
Am
CHRISTINE
Ah!
F
Ah!
Am
Ah!
Am
Ah!
6/4

THE MUSIC OF THE NIGHT

Music by ANDREW LLOYD WEBBER
Lyrics by CHARLES HART
Additional lyrics by RICHARD STILGOE

night un-furls its splen-dour; grasp it, sense it, trem-u-lous and ten-der.
Turn your face a-way from the gar-ish light of day, turn your thoughts a-way from cold, un-feel-ing
light and lis-ten to the mu sic of the night. Close your eyes and sur-ren-der to your
dark-est dreams! Purge your thoughts of the life you knew be - fore! Close your

rall.
rit.
a tempo
rall.
Ab
Ab7
Db
Fm
C
mp
F
Db
Ab/Db
Db
Ab/Db
Db
Ab/Db
p
Gb
Ab
Gb
Db
Gb
Db
Gb
Cb
Gb
Db/Ab
Gb/Ab
Ab7
eyes, let your spi - rit start to soar and you'll live as you've nev - er lived be -
fore. Soft - ly, deft - ly, mu - sic shall ca - ress you. Hear it, feel it,
se - cret - ly po - sess you. O - pen up your mind, let your fan - ta - sies un - wind in this
dark - ness which you know you can - not fight, the dark - ness of the mu - sic of the

a tempo
Db
B
E
night. Let your mind start a jour-ney through a strange, new world; leave all
f
A
Eb
Ab
Ab7
rall.
thoughts of the life you knew be - fore. Let your soul take you where you long to
Db
molto rit.
Fm
C
F
be! On - ly then can you be - long to me.
ff
mp
a tempo
Db
Ab/Db
Db
Ab/Db
Db
Ab/Db
Gb/Db
Ab/Db
Float - ing, fall - ing, sweet in-tox-i-ca - tion. Touch me, trust me, sa-vour each sen-sa - tion.
mp

Let the dream be-gin, let your dark-er side give in to the pow-er of the mu-sic that I write, the
pow-er of the mu-sic of the night.
You a-lone can make my song take
flight, help me make the mu-sic of the night.
rall. a tempo
rall. a tempo
rall. lento
mf
ff
mp
pp

PRIMA DONNA

Music by ANDREW LLOYD WEBBER
Lyrics by CHARLES HART
Additional lyrics by RICHARD STILGOE

C/E   B♭   G   C   TOGETHER
all a - dore you. Pri - ma Don - na, en -
ANDRÉ   FIRMIN   C7   F
-chant us once a - gain! Think of your muse and of the queues round the thea - tre!
Dm7   G   G/F   C/E   Am
TOGETHER
Can you de - ny us the tri - umph in store? Sing,
Dm11   G7   C
RAOUL
Pri - ma Don - na, once more!
Christ - ine spoke of an

CARLOTTA
F
Pri - ma Don - na, your song shall live a - gain, you took a snub, but there's a
an - gel.
Dm
C
Gm
C7
C/B♭
pub - lic who needs you.___ Think of their cry of un -
F/A
Dm
B♭
F/A
E♭
-dy - ing___ sup - port, fol - low where the lime - light leads you!
C
F
___ Pri - ma Don - na, your song shall nev - er die, you'll sing a -

F7   B♭
-gain   and   to   un - end - ing   o - va - tion._____

Gm   C7   C/B♭   F/A   Dm
Think   how   you'll   shine   in   that   fi - nal_____   en - core;   sing;

Gm11   C7   F   F7
Pri - ma   Don - na,   once   more!________________________

B♭
ANDRÉ & FIRMIN
Who'd be-lieve a di-va hap-py to re-lieve a   cho-rus girl who's gone and   slept with the pa - tron?_

Gm
F
Raoul and the soub-rette en-twined in love's du-et; al-though he may de-mur he must have been with her. You'd
Cm
F
B♭/D
Gm
nev-er get a-way with all this in a play, but if it's loud-ly sung and in a for-eign tongue, it's
E♭
B♭/D
A♭
F
just the sort of sto-ry au-dien-ces a-dore, in fact a per-fect op-era.
B♭
Pri - ma Don - na, the world is at your feet, a na - tion

B♭7   E♭
waits and how it hates to be cheat - ed.
Cm   F   B♭/D   rit.   Gm
optional
ALL
Light up the stage with that age old rap - port; sing,
ff
Cm11   F7   a tempo   B♭ A G♯ G F♭ F
Pri - ma Don - na, once more!
E F F♯ G G♯ A B♭ A G♯ G F♯ F E F F♯ G G♯ A

ALL I ASK OF YOU

Music by ANDREW LLOYD WEBBER
Lyrics by CHARLES HART
Additional lyrics by RICHARD STILGOE

D♭maj7   G♭6   C♭   A♭/C
here,   with you,   be - side you,   to   guard you   and   to guide you.

D♭   B♭m7   E♭m7   A♭   D♭/F   B♭m7
CHRISTINE
Say   you   love me   ev -'ry   wak - ing   mo - ment,   turn   my head with talk of

E♭m7   E♭m7/A♭   D♭   B♭m7   E♭m7   A♭
sum - mer - time.   Say   you   need me with you   now   and   al - ways;

D♭/F   G♭   D♭/A♭   rit.   E♭m/A♭   A♭6   E♭m7/A♭
pro - mise me   that   all   you say   is   true,   that's all   I   ask of

a tempo
D♭   RAOUL   D♭maj7   G♭6
Let me be your shel-ter, let me be your light; you're safe, no one will find you, your
you.
C♭   A♭/C   D♭   CHRISTINE
fears are far be-hind you. All I want is free-dom, a world with no more night; and
D♭maj7   G♭6   C♭   A♭/C   RAOUL D♭   B♭m7
you, al-ways be-side me, to hold me and to hide me. Then say you'll share with me one
E♭m7   A♭   D♭/F   B♭m7   E♭m7   A♭   A♭6 A♭7
love, one life-time; let me lead you from your so-li-tude._

Say you need me with you, here be-side you, a-ny-where you go, let me go too,
rit. molto rit. a tempo
CHRISTINE
Christ-ine,___ that's all I ask of you. Say you'll share with me one
love one life-time; say the word and I will fol-low you.___
TOGETHER
Share each day with me, each night, each morn-ing.
CHRISTINE
Say you love me!
RAOUL
You know I
rit.

49

molto rit.
RAOUL & CHRISTINE
do. Love me, that's all I ask of you.
largo
UNISON
A-ny-where you go, let me go
molto rit.
RAOUL & CHRISTINE
too; love me that's all I ask of you.

MASQUERADE

Music by ANDREW LLOYD WEBBER
Lyrics by CHARLES HART
Additional lyrics by RICHARD STILGOE

C   G   C   G/C   Dm/C
world will nev - er find you.   Mas-quer-ade,______   ev-ery   face a diff-erent shade,
F   C
mas - quer - ade,______ look a - round there's an - oth - er mask be-hind you. Flash of
C   F/C
mauve, splash of puce, fool and king, ghoul and goose, green and black, queen and priest, trace of rouge, face of beast.
F   C/G   G
Fa - ces, take your turn, take a ride on the mer - ry-go round
In an in - hu - man

C
F/C
gold, thigh of blue, true is false, who is who, curl of lip, swirl of gown, ace of hearts, face of clown.
race.
mp
F
C/G
G
RAOUL & CHRISTINE
Fa - ces, drink it in, drink it up, till you've drowned in the light, in the sound, but who can name the
C
ALL
G/C
Dm7/C
F/C
face? Mas-que-rade,___ grin-ning yel-lows, spin-ning reds. Mas-quer-ade,___ take your fill, let the
mf
2/4
4/4
C
G
C
G/C
Dm7/C
spec - ta-cle as-tound you. Mas-quer-ade,___ burn-ing glan-ces, turn-ing heads,
2/4
4/4

mas - quer - ade, stop and stare at the sea of smiles a - round you.
Mas - quer - ade, seeth - ing sha - dows, breath - ing lies,
mas - quer - ade, you can fool a - ny
friend who ev - er knew you.
Mas - quer - ade, leer - ing sa - tyrs, peer - ing eyes,
mas - quer - ade, run and hide, but a face will still pur - sue you. What a
CARLOTTA

Db
PIANGI   ANDRÉ   FIRMIN
night,   what   a   crowd,   makes   you   glad,   makes   you   proud,   all   the
mp

Gb/Db
CARLOTTA   MEG & GIRY
crème   de   la   crème,   watch - ing   us,   watch - ing   them,
And   all   our   fears   are   in   the

Gb
ANDRÉ   PIANGI   CARLOTTA   ANDRÉ   Db/Ab   Ab   FIRMIN   CARLOTTA
three____ months of re - lief,   of de - light,   of El - y - si - an peace.   No more
past.   And we can breathe at

Db
PIANGI   GIRY   ANDRÉ   Gb/Db   FIRMIN   CARLOTTA & PIANGI
notes, no more ghost, here's a health, here's a toast to a   pros-per-ous year, to our friends who are here.
last.   And may our
mp

G♭
GIRY
What a change, what a bles - sed re - lease and what a mas - quer-
splen - dour nev - er fade.
D♭/A♭
FIRMIN & ANDRÉ
A♭
GIRY

poco meno mosso
D♭
C
ALL
G/C
Dm⁷/C
- ade!
Mas - quer - ade,____ pa - per fa - ces on par - ade,
f

F
C
G
mas - quer - ade,____ hide your face, so the world will nev - er find you.

C
G/B
Dm⁷
F
Mas - quer - ade,____ ev - ery face a diff - erent shade,____ mas - quer - ade,____ look a - round, there's an-
f

C   B♭   E♭   B♭/E♭   Fm7/E♭
-oth - er mask be-hind you.   Mas-quer-ade,_____ burn-ing glan-ces, turn-ing heads.
ff
A♭   E♭   B♭13 B♭7
Mas - quer-ade,_______ stop and stare at the sea of smiles a-round you.
E♭   B♭/D   Fm
Mas - quer - ade,________ grin - ning yel - lows, spin - ning reds,
A♭   rit.   Cm   Cm Bm B♭m Am A♭m
mas-quer-ade,____ take your fill, let the spec - ta-cle as-tound you.
fff

57

THE FAIRGROUND

Composed by ANDREW LLOYD WEBBER

più animato
ff
rall.
61

JOURNEY TO THE CEMETERY

Composed by ANDREW LLOYD WEBBER

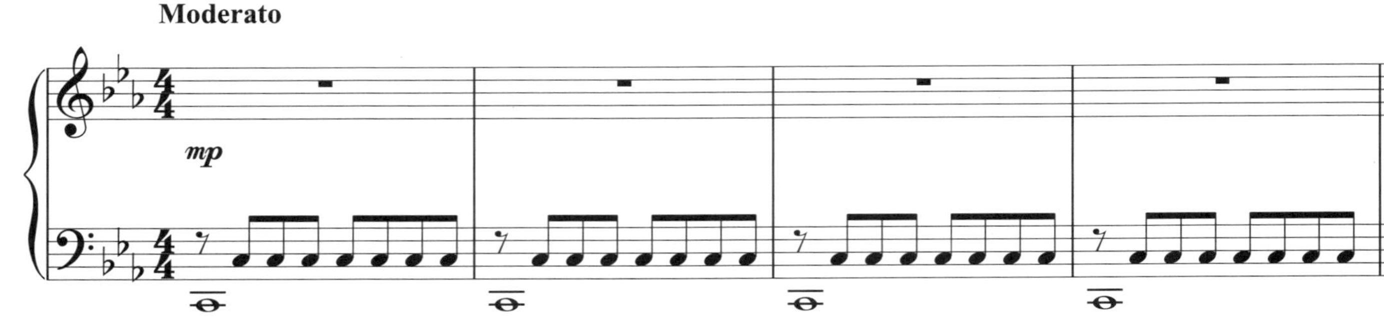

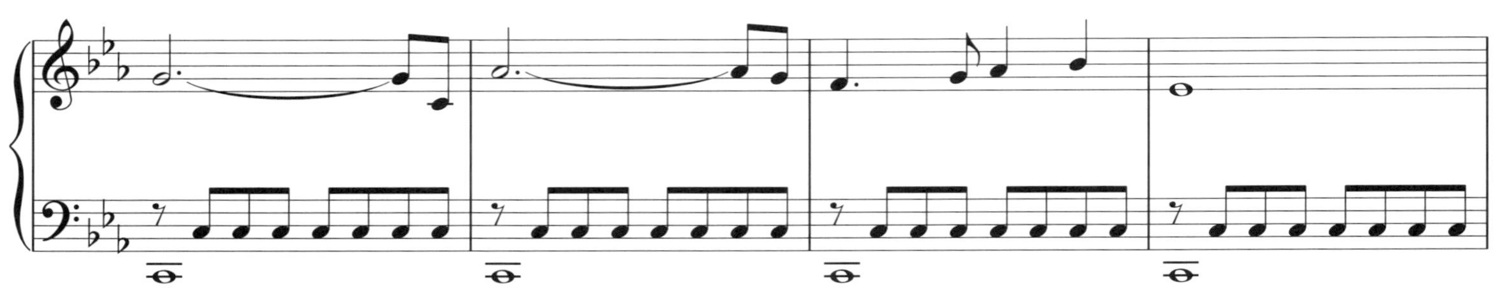

f marcato
f

WISHING YOU WERE SOMEHOW HERE AGAIN

Music by ANDREW LLOYD WEBBER
Lyrics by CHARLES HART
Additional lyrics by RICHARD STILGOE

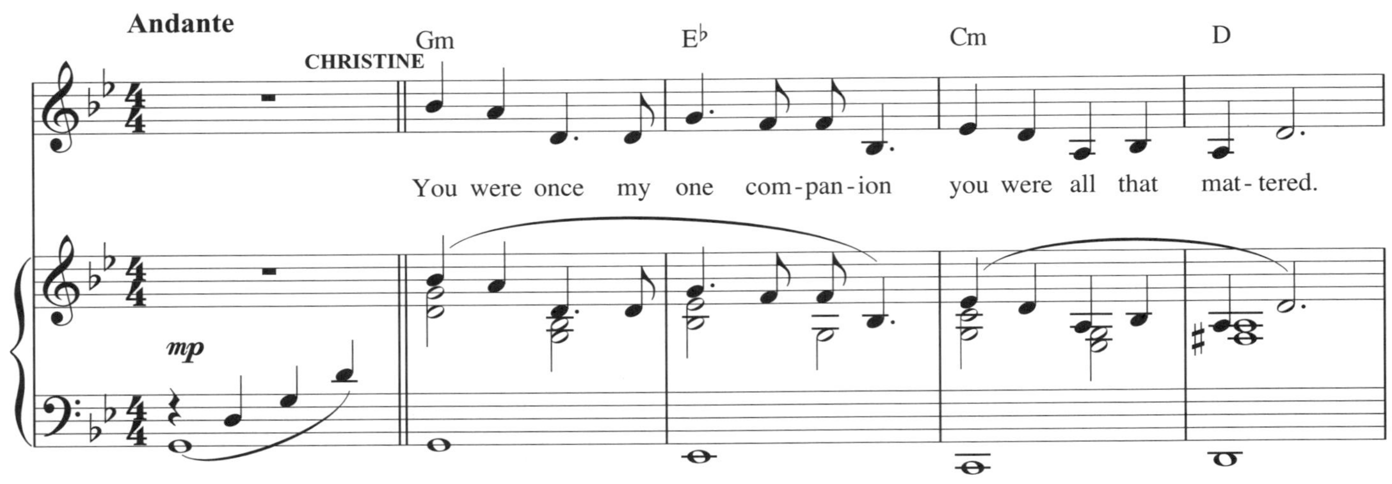

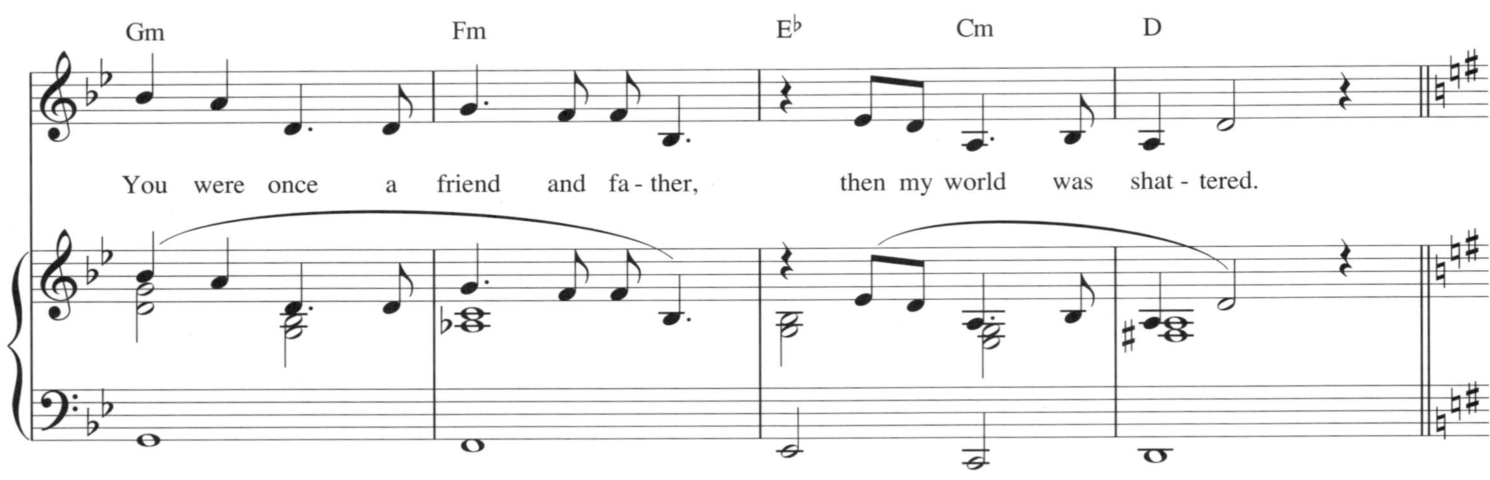

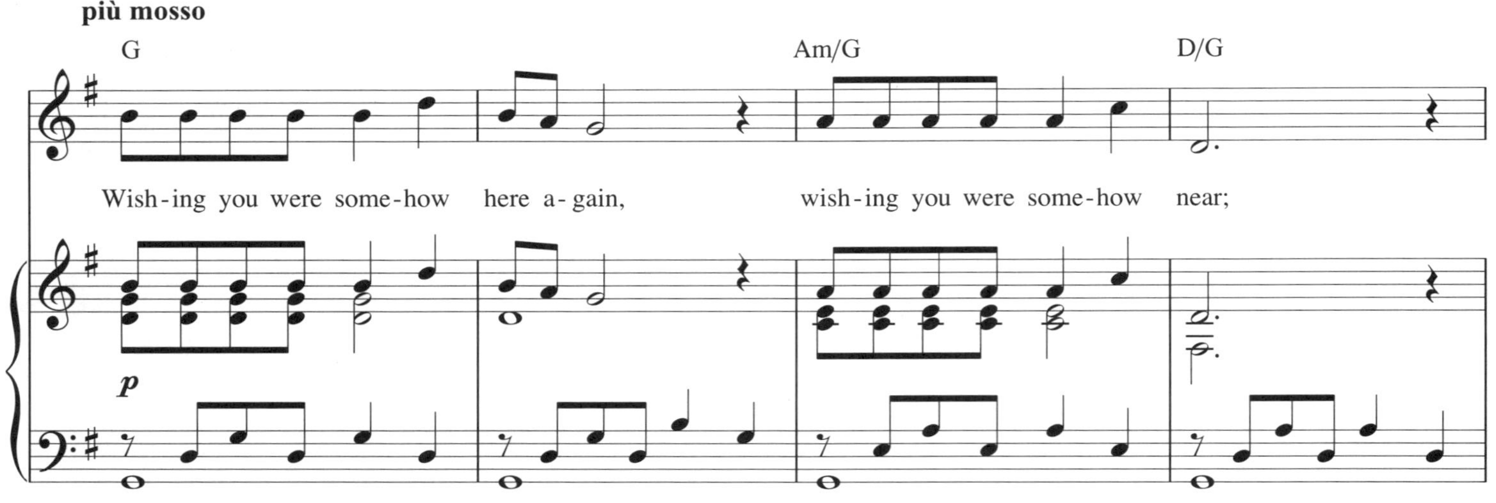

C
D/C
Bm7
Em
Bm7
Em
D
D7
some-times it seemed   if I just dreamed,   some-how you would   be here.
G
Am/G
D/G
mp
Wish-ing I could hear your   voice a-gain,   know-ing that I nev - er   would,
C
D/C
Bm7
Em
Bm7
Em
D
dream-ing of you   won't help me to do   all that you dreamed   I could.
poco meno mosso
Gm
Eb
Cm
D
mp
Pass - ing bells   and sculp - ted an-gels,   cold   and   mon - u - men - tal,

seem for you the wrong com-pan-ions; you were warm and gen - tle.
Too ma-ny years fight-ing back tears, why can't the past just die?
Wish-ing you were some - how here a - gain, know-ing we must say good -

a tempo
F7   Eb F/Eb Dm7 Gm Dm7 Gm
bye.   Try to for-give,   teach me to live,   give me the strength to
mf
3   3   3   3

rit.   a tempo
F7   Bb F/Bb Eb/Bb F/Bb Bb F/Bb
try.   No more me-mo-ries, no more si - lent tears, no more gaz-ing a-cross the
f

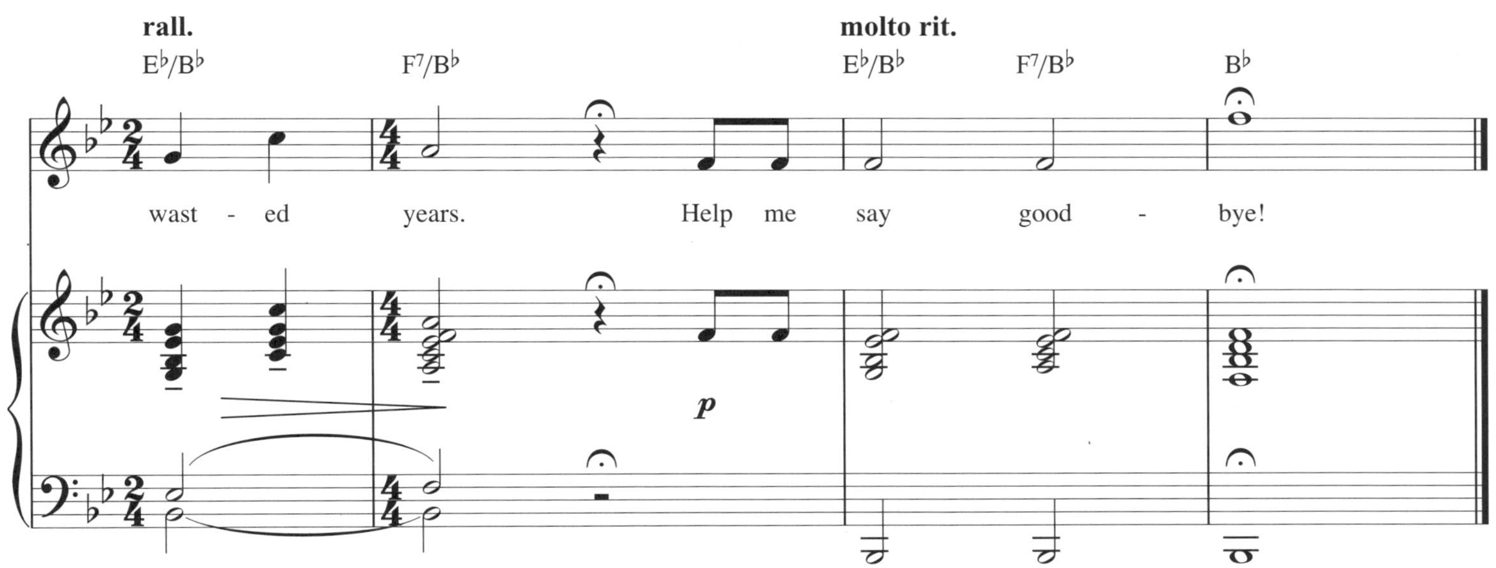
rall.   molto rit.
Eb/Bb F7/Bb Eb/Bb F7/Bb Bb
wast - ed   years.   Help me say   good - bye!
p

THE POINT OF NO RETURN

Music by ANDREW LLOYD WEBBER
Lyrics by CHARLES HART
Additional lyrics by RICHARD STILGOE

Andante (♩.)

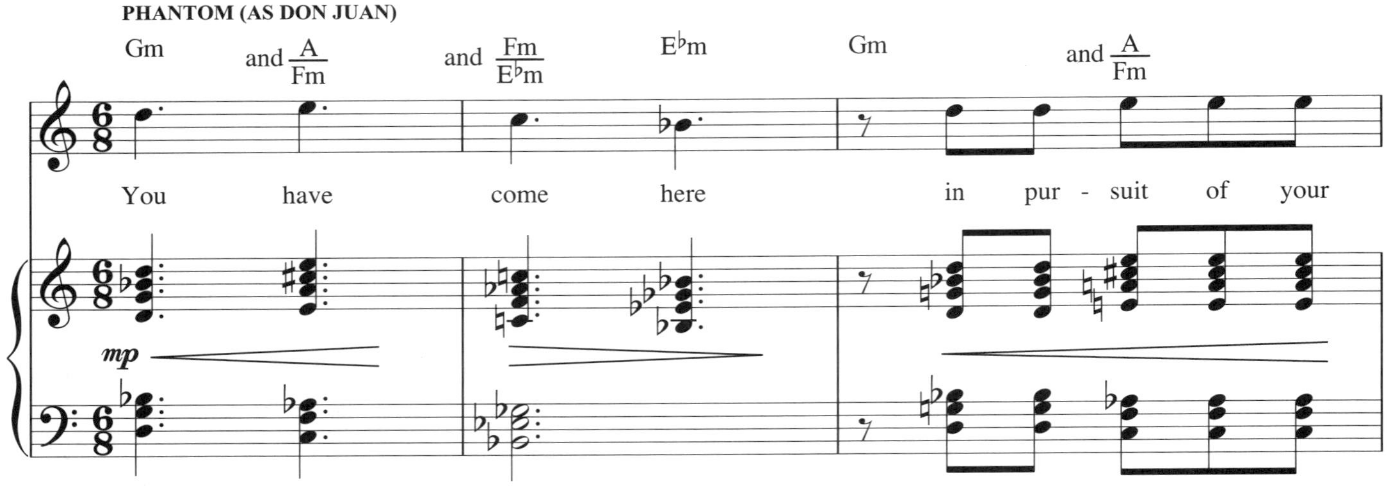

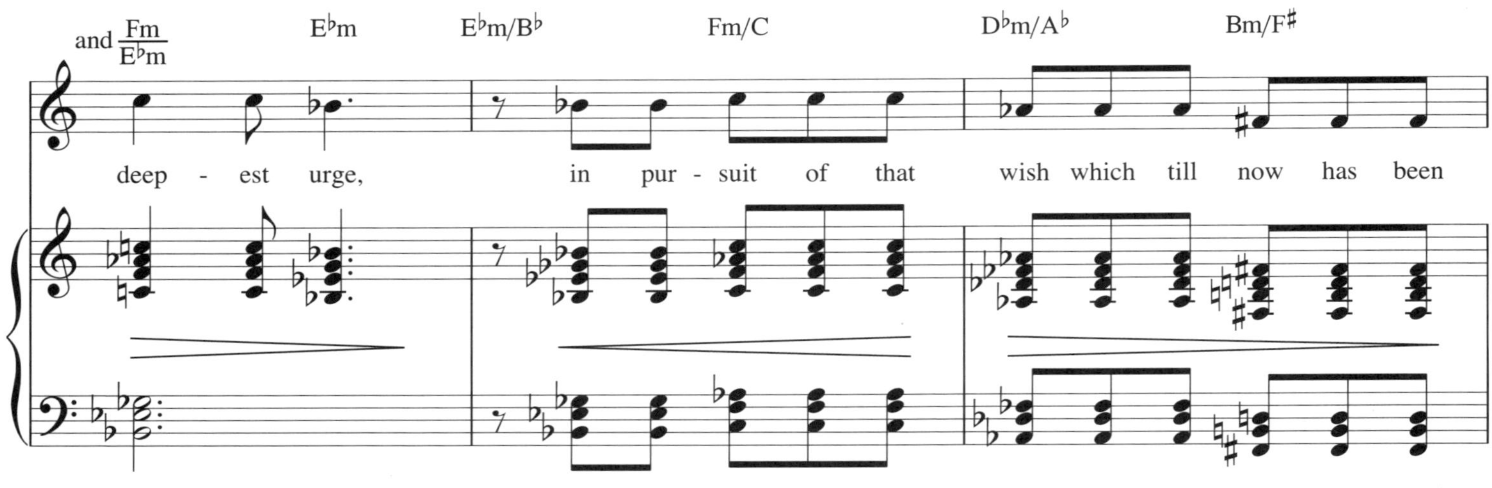

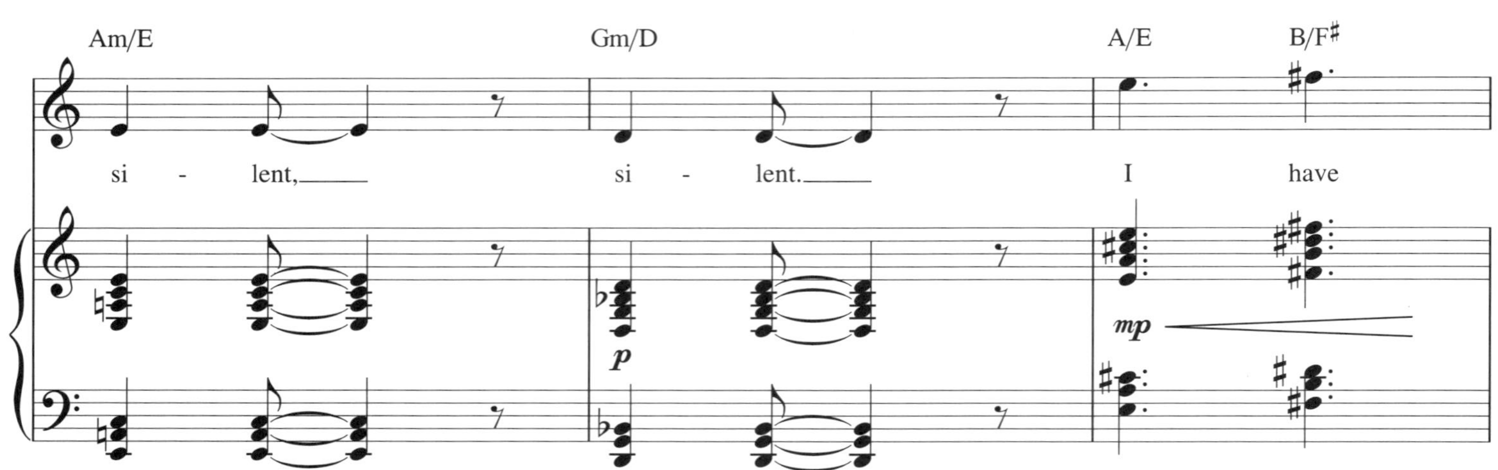

A♭/E♭ G♭m/D♭ A/E B/F# A♭/E♭ G♭m/D♭
brought you that our pas - sions may fuse and merge.
F#m/C# G#m/D# Em/B Dm/A Em/B F#m/C# G#m/D#
In your mind you've al - rea - dy suc-cumbed to me, dropped all de - fen - ces, com-
Em/B Dm/A Cm/G B♭m/F
-plete - ly suc-cumbed to me, now you are here with me, no se - cond thoughts, you've de-
rit.
A♭m/E♭ Gm/D
- ci - ded,___ de - ci - ded.___
p
4/4

Allegretto
Past the point of no re-turn, no back-ward glan-ces; the games of make be-lieve are at an end.
più mosso
Past all thought of "if" or "when", no use re--sis-ting, a-ban-don thought and let the dream de-scend.

What rag - ing fire shall flood the soul? What rich de - sire un - locks its
door? What sweet se - duc - tion lies be - fore us?
Past the point of no re - turn, the fi - nal thre - shold, what
warm un - spo - ken se - crets will we learn be - yond the point of

CHRISTINE (AS AMINTA)
a tempo 1°
G♭   C⁷   Fm   Gm   and A/Fm   and Fm/E♭m   E♭m
no re - turn? You have brought me
Gm   and A/Fm   and Fm/E♭m   E♭m   E♭m/B♭   Fm/C   D♭m/A♭   Bm/F♯
to that mo-ment where words run dry, to that mo-ment where speech dis-ap-pears in-to
rit.
Am/E   Gm/D   a tempo   A/E   B/F♯   A♭/E♭   G♭m/D♭
si - lence,___ si - lence.___ I have come here
A/E   B/F♯   A♭/E♭   G♭m/D♭   F♯m/C♯   G♯m/D♯   Em/B   Dm/A   Em/B
hard-ly know-ing the rea-son why, in my mind I've al-rea-dy i-ma-gined our
mf
mp
mf

F#m/C#   G#m/D#   Em/B   Dm/A   Cm/G
bo - dies en - twin - ing, de - fence - less and si - lent and now I am here with you,
rit.
B♭m/F   A♭m/E♭   Gm/D
no se - cond thoughts, I've de - ci - ded,__ de - ci - ded.__
poco accel.
Fm   C⁷/F   Fm
Past_______ the point of no re - turn, no go - ing
F   D♭   E♭⁷   A♭
back now, our pas - sion play has now at last be - gun.
Ped.   *   Ped.   *

Past all thought of right or wrong,
one fi - nal ques - tion; how long should we two
wait be-fore we're one? When will the blood be - gin to
race? The sleep - ing bud burst in - to bloom? When will the flames at last con -

rit.
a tempo
Gm7b5
C7
Gm/D
TOGETHER
-sume
us?
Past the point of
f
Ped.
Ped.
D7
Gm/D
G/D
rit.
G7
no re-turn,
the fi-nal thre-shold,
the
ff
Eb
F7
Bb
bridge is crossed, so stand and watch it burn. We've
Eb
molto rit.
Ab
D7
Gm
passed the point of no re - turn.
mf
p

LEARN TO BE LONELY

Music by ANDREW LLOYD WEBBER
Lyrics by CHARLES HART

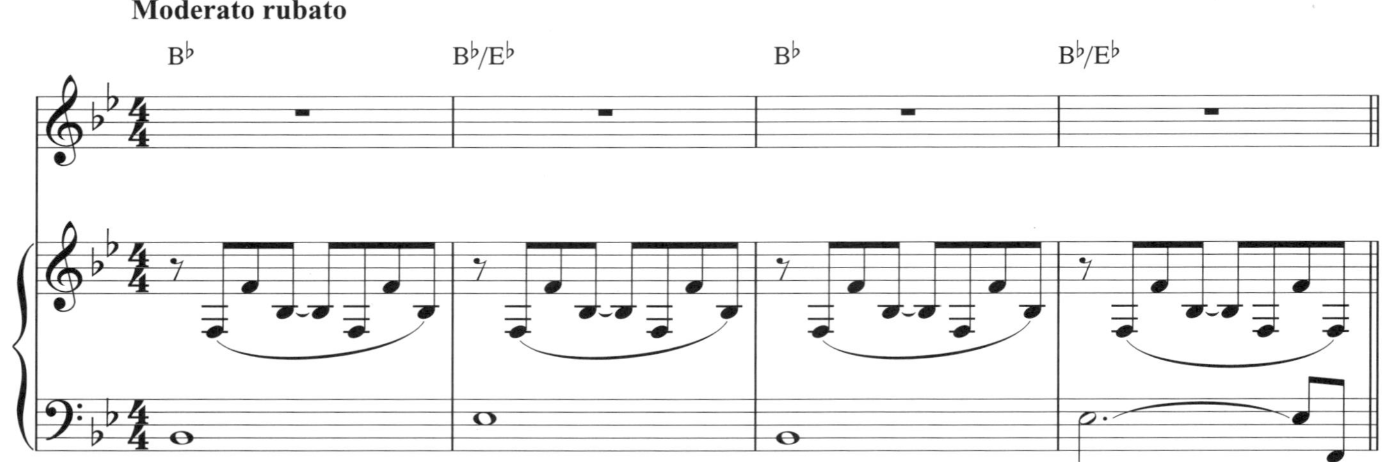

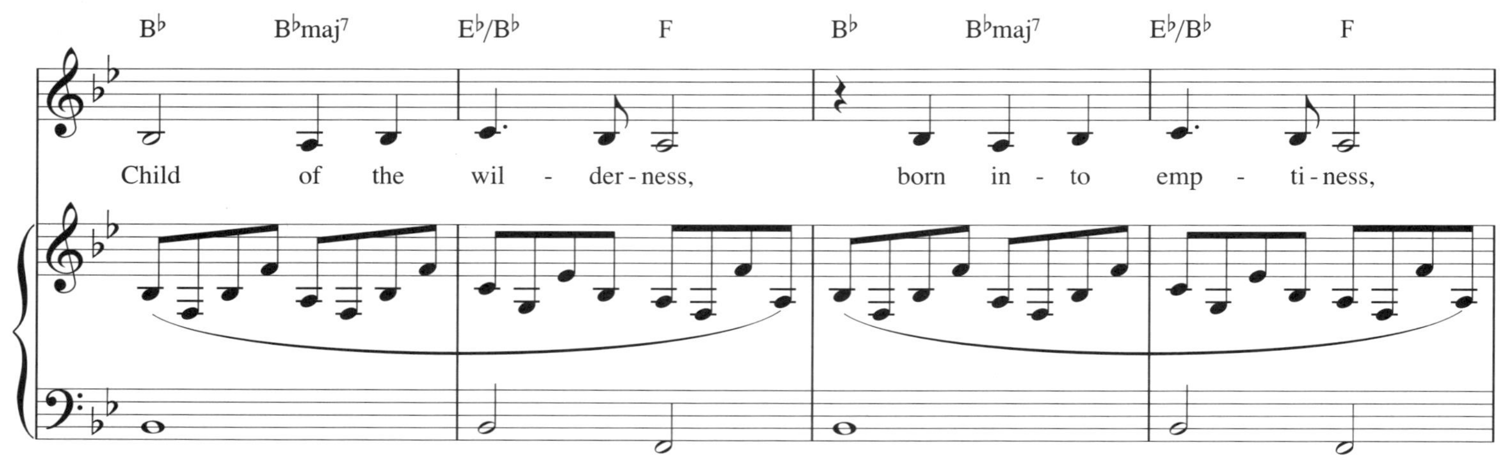

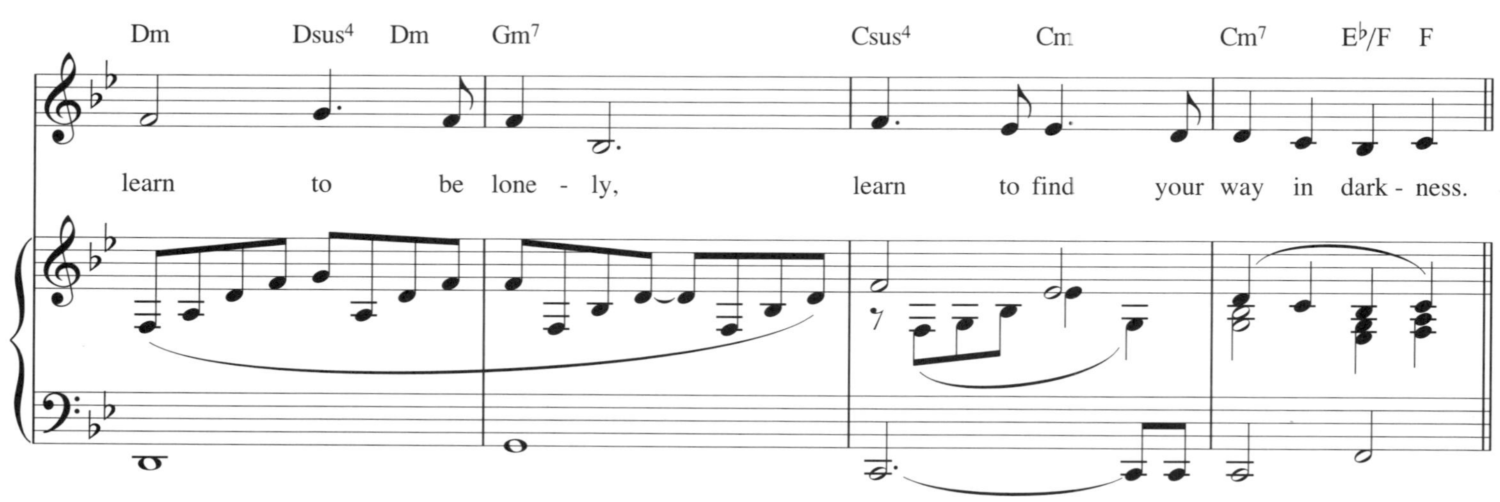

Who will be there for you? Com - fort and care for you?
Learn to be lone - ly, learn to be your one com - pan - ion.
Ne - ver dream that out in the world there are arms to hold you. You've
al - ways known your heart was on its own. So

laugh in your lone - li - ness. Child of the wil - der - ness.
Learn to be lone - ly, learn how to love life that is lived a -
- lone.
Learn to be lone - ly. Life can be lived, life can be loved a - lone.

Piano Vocal Selections
오페라의 유령 오리지널 사운드트랙 [한국어판]

초판 제1쇄 발행 2006년 11월 10일

펴낸곳/모노폴리
펴낸이/강정미

등록번호 제2005-48호 등록날짜 2005년 8월 9일
주소/121-704 서울시 마포구 도화2동 36번지 고려빌딩 822호
전화/02)3272-6692 팩스/02)3272-6693
http//www.monopolymusic.co.kr

ISBN 89-91952-00-3 13670
값 10,000원